Clowns' Play

By
REGINALD F. BAIN

A participation play for young people
to be performed by adults

THE DRAMATIC PUBLISHING COMPANY

*** NOTICE ***

The amateur and stock acting rights to this work are controlled exclusively by THE DRAMATIC PUBLISHING COMPANY without whose permission in writing no performance of it may be given. Royalty fees are given in our current catalogue and are subject to change without notice. Royalty must be paid every time a play is performed whether or not it is presented for profit and whether or not admission is charged. A play is performed anytime it is acted before an audience. All inquiries concerning amateur and stock rights should be addressed to:

DRAMATIC PUBLISHING
P. O. Box 129, Woodstock, Illinois 60098.

COPYRIGHT LAW GIVES THE AUTHOR OR THE AUTHOR'S AGENT THE EXCLUSIVE RIGHT TO MAKE COPIES. This law provides authors with a fair return for their creative efforts. Authors earn their living from the royalties they receive from book sales and from the performance of their work. Conscientious observance of copyright law is not only ethical, it encourages authors to continue their creative work. This work is fully protected by copyright. No alterations, deletions or substitutions may be made in the work without the prior written consent of the publisher. No part of this work may be reproduced or transmitted in any form or by any means, electronic or mechanical, including photocopy, recording, videotape, film, or any information storage and retrieval system, without permission in writing from the publisher. It may not be performed either by professionals or amateurs without payment of royalty. All rights, including but not limited to the professional, motion picture, radio, television, videotape, foreign language, tabloid, recitation, lecturing, publication, and reading are reserved. *On all programs this notice should appear:*

"Produced by special arrangement with
THE DRAMATIC PUBLISHING COMPANY of Woodstock, Illinois"

©MCMLXXXI by
REGINALD F. BAIN

Printed in the United States of America
All Rights Reserved
(CLOWNS' PLAY)

ISBN 0-87129-424-9

CLOWNS' PLAY was first presented under the title *Jack and the Beanstalk* by the Notre Dame-Saint Mary's Theatre in the Little Theatre (Moreau Hall) on the Saint Mary's College campus, Notre Dame, Indiana. The production was directed by Janet Wilson with the following cast:

Boffo	Terence Kennedy
Mustard	Aubrey Payne
Trinket	Kathrene Wales
Ruffina	Nancy Syburg
Musculo	Dan Daily
Doxy	Katharine Burke
Moxy	Kathryn Gaffney
Scrappy	Dan Deziel

CLOWNS' PLAY
A Participation Play
For Four Men and Four Women

CHARACTERS

BOFFO .... the con man

MUSTARD .... narrator, Farmer Brown, golden hen

TRINKET .... con man's accomplice, singing harp

RUFFINA .... giant's wife

MUSCULO .... the giant

DOXY .... Bessie the cow

MOXY .... Jack's mother

SCRAPPY .... Jack

SCENE: A bare stage with cyclorama. There are two signs on easels placed at the proscenium. They read: "Show Today — Jack and the Beanstalk"

CLOWNS' PLAY

BOFFO has been ushering with the other CLOWNS. When it is time for the play to begin, he makes his way to the stage and the other CLOWNS distribute themselves in the aisles of the theatre. As BOFFO reaches the stage he signals for the house lights to dim to half and the stage lights to be brought up. A fanfare is heard. BOFFO moves C to introduce the play.

BOFFO. Ladies and gentlemen! Young people of all ages! The — (Name of group.) — theatre is pleased to present an exciting new version of that age-old tale — *Jack and the Beanstalk*. (Other CLOWNS applaud.) We are most fortunate to have with us to play this wonderful story a troupe of actors from . . .

MUSTARD (interrupting from audience). Wait! Wait a minute! Stop!

BOFFO. What's the meaning of this? Who's interrupting our show? (He sees MUSTARD.) Oh, it's you. What do you think you're doing? (MUSTARD has climbed up onto the stage. BOFFO crosses to him angrily.) You boob! (He bops MUSTARD over the head and MUSTARD falls to the floor.)

MUSTARD. Wait! I've got something to tell you. We just —

BOFFO. No, we can't wait. These people want to see our show. (Back to audience.) Now, as I was saying . . .

MUSTARD. But, I must tell you . . .

BOFFO (bopping MUSTARD again). Silence! (Back to audience.) Please excuse this bumbling buzzard! Now, back to my introduction . . . (MUSTARD makes to say something but thinks better of it as BOFFO raises his hand to hit him again. Resigned, MUSTARD moves away

and sits on stage.)
MUSTARD. Okay! Go on . . . Dunderhead!
BOFFO. What! (He starts to go after MUSTARD but the other CLOWNS rush to stage and intervene.)
CLOWNS (general reaction). Stop it, both of you. Go on, introduce the show! (Etc.)
BOFFO (composing himself and returning to C). Well, as I was saying before I was so rudely interrupted by that crass, crazy, crude . . . (His anger returns.)
CLOWNS (together). Introduce the show!
BOFFO (to audience). Sorry. (Back to introduction.) It is with great pride that we of the — (Name of group.) — theatre bring you a special performance of *Jack and the Beanstalk* performed by a traveling troupe of actors all the way from Bumble Bee, Arizona. We give you — The Bumblebee Barnstormers! (Fanfare. No one enters. BOFFO is confused. MUSTARD knowingly gloats. The other CLOWNS look at one another wondering what has happened. BOFFO decides to try again.) The Bumblebee Barnstormers! (Fanfare. Again no response. CLOWNS whisper to one another. BOFFO whispers to TRINKET to go off and see what's the matter. She does so. MUSTARD continues to be amused. BOFFO returns to the audience a bit shook.) Well . . . um . . . I can't imagine what's holding things up . . . um . . . (An idea.) Maybe, if we all introduce the actors together, they'd come out. All right, now everyone . . . let's try introducing them together. Ready. The Bumblebee Barnstormers! Again, louder — The Bumblebee Barnstormers!

(TRINKET returns, obviously distrubed. BOFFO runs to her.)

BOFFO. What's the matter? Where are they? Aren't they ready yet?

CLOWNS' PLAY

Page 7

TRINKET (can hardly get it out). They . . . they . . . they aren't here!

CLOWNS (general reaction). What happened? I don't understand. (Etc.)

BOFFO (sitting on stage next to MUSTARD). What are we going to do?

MUSTARD (he now has the upper hand). That's what I was trying to tell you. But, of course, you wouldn't listen. Just as the house lights were going down to start the show, I got a phone call on the phone out in the lobby. The Barnstormer's van broke down on the highway and they're not going to be able to make it for this performance. (There is general dismay.)

MOXY. Oh, dear, we don't have a show!

MUSCULO. These people paid their money. We promised them *Jack and the Beanstalk*.

SCRAPPY. Maybe we'll have to return the money.

DOXY. Maybe they could come back another day.

MUSTARD. No. No. Wait, all of you. What's the matter with you? You're clowns, aren't you? We call ourselves the — (Name of group.) — theatre, don't we? We don't need to depend on another group to do the show. We can do it ourselves. (General reaction of doubt from the others.)

BOFFO. But you can't do a play you haven't rehearsed, you raspy rapscallion. We were hired as ushers. We're clowns, not actors. Clowns do their bits of business and make people happy. (He demonstrates with a bit of business like jumping up, touching heels and falling on the floor.) But clowns don't act characters in plays. Besides, we don't have a script.

MUSTARD. That just shows what you know. You're new at being a clown. I've been around awhile and I can tell you that actors and clowns are very much alike. Look around you. Look at those faces. Each one is different. Each one is a character — an individual, a person. Look at them. (He goes to each and introduces them.) Trinket and Scrappy — playful children ready to trick you without warning.

(TRINKET moves to BOFFO and distracts him while SCRAPPY moves around behind him. When SCRAPPY is down on his hands and knees behind BOFFO, TRINKET pushes BOFFO over SCRAPPY. BOFFO ends up on the floor.)

MUSTARD. And you, Boffo, always ready for a good fight.

(MUSTARD tosses BOFFO a stick which becomes a "sword." They fight and MUSTARD disarms him. BOFFO again ends up on the floor.)

MUSTARD. Ah, yes, and then there's Musculo, the magnificent would-be strongman — and his assistant Ruffina.

(RUFFINA hands MUSCULO a piece of "steel" to bend. He bends it after some great effort. He bows, accepts the applause of the group. As he hands the "steel" bar back to RUFFINA it flops over and we see that is was obviously a phony.)

MUSTARD. Look out there! Here come those two schemers — Moxy and Doxy. They're liable to pull anything, watch out!

(One of the two girls brings out a hose from the wings and points it at the audience threateningly. The other brings out a wooden bucket to fill. They "fill" bucket, look at each other, and decide to throw contents at audience. They make a couple of false starts and finally throw

CLOWNS' PLAY

confetti-filled bucket at audience.)

MUSTARD. So, you see, Boffo, we all have our roles to play. We are actors, too.
BOFFO (not so sure). Okay . . . okay . . . But what about a script?
MUSCULO. Let's improvise. (General agreement from the others.)
BOFFO. That's a word I don't know. What's it mean?
MUSTARD. I bet our friends in the audience know that word. (To audience.) Does anyone out there know what "to improvise" means? (CLOWNS should help to solicit responses from audience until definition is obtained. Try to use audience's suggestions repeating them as they are brought up.) Right. That's it. To improvise means to make it up as you go along. We don't need a script. We all know the story of *Jack and the Beanstalk*.

(MOXY runs offstage and comes back immediately with an over-sized book. *Jack and the Beanstalk* is clearly visible in large letters on the cover.)

MOXY. I've got the book. We can use this to follow the story.
MUSTARD. Good. And I bet all these young people know it well enough to help us — if we run into trouble. (To audience.) Will you help us? (Other CLOWNS ask also. Audience will say yes.) Good! Now, Actors . . . (He says "actors" with relish.) Let's improvise. (The CLOWNS gather around MUSTARD, who has opened the book and is kneeling over it.)
CLOWNS (general response). I'll play Jack . . . I want to be the giant . . . giant's wife . . . the cow . . . (Etc.)
MUSTARD (quieting them). Wait! Since I am your leader, I will decide who plays which role. It is difficult to

improvise without a leader or director to make some decisions. Otherwise we'll have utter chaos and we won't entertain our friends out there. All right now, everybody line up. (The CLOWNS do so, fighting for spots.) Stop it! Let's see . . . (Thinking out loud.) We need a Jack . . . hmm . . . (To audience.) What do you think Jack should be like? (Solicits responses from audience.) Yes . . . young . . . oh, that's good . . . yes . . . (He uses the suggestions from audience. Things like "able to climb beanstalk," and "quick enough to run from giant" will do. While this is going on, other CLOWNS are "acting" the part of Jack.) Good. Good. Yes, Jack certainly must do that. Okay . . . now I would say . . . (Looking over line of CLOWNS.) I would say that . . . (Kidding them.) Musculo the Magnificent should play Jack. Don't you think he's just right? (The audience should obviously disagree.) No? Well, how about Scrappy? (The audience should agree.) Now, how about the giant? What should he be like? (Responding to audience as before.) Yes . . . yes . . . The giant should be the strongest person. Do you see anyone up here who could play the giant? Yes, of course — Musculo the Magnificent. (MUSCULO is quite pleased.) Now, what about Jack's mother? That's hard. We have four women here, each of whom could easily do it. (Thinking again.) I'll tell you what . . . I'll write their names on these pieces of paper and put them in this hat. One of you can pick out the name of the person who will play Jack's mother. (MUSTARD goes into the audience and selects someone to pick one piece of paper out of the hat. The child will pull out the name of "Moxy.") Moxy — it's you. Good, it is decided then that Moxy will play Jack's mother. Now, there is just one more character to be selected. Who's that, do you think? Yes . . . yes . . . the cow! We must choose Jack's cow — a most important character in the story. (Thinking again.)

CLOWNS' PLAY
Page 11

Gee, how shall we choose the actor to play the cow? (By this time the young people in the audience should be well into the game of casting the play and suggestions should be somewhat spontaneous. It should not take too much prodding to get them to come up with the idea of having a "mooing" contest.) Good idea! Yes, that's it — a mooing contest. Let's have each of the actors who have not yet been given a part make the sound of a cow and you select the best cow sound. (To CLOWNS.) Now each of you show me what Jack's cow sounds like. First you, Boffo. (BOFFO makes the sound of a donkey.) Oh, come on, that's certainly not it. Ruffina? (RUFFINA makes the sound of a rooster.) Oh, dear! How about you, Trinket? (TRINKET makes the sound of a kitten.) I don't believe it. Are you people pulling my leg? Doxy, I hope you won't let me down. (DOXY does not let him down. She makes the sound of a soothing cow's "moo-moo.") Well, there seems to be no doubt that Doxy should play Jack's cow Bessie. All right, everyone, let's improvise. I will pick the other characters as we go along.

BOFFO. Wait!

CLOWNS (general reaction). What is it now? What do you want? Not again. Let's get started. (Etc.)

BOFFO. We don't have a set. The Barnstormers were supposed to bring it with them.

MUSTARD. Boffo is right. We need some kind of a set. (TRINKET finds a block in the wings and brings in on stage.)

TRINKET. How about this? (RUFFINA pulls in a trunk from offstage.)

RUFFINA. Here are all our clown props. These might be useful.

MUSTARD (going to trunk). Yes, the costumes and properties which we use as clowns will help us play the story of *Jack and the Beanstalk*. (A thought.) Oh, dear, I just thought of something. What are we going to do for a beanstalk? You can't play the story without a beanstalk.

MUSCULO (dragging in a ladder). How about this?

MUSTARD (inspecting the ladder). Great idea! (He moves the ladder to the wings so that one half of the ladder is offstage and the other half on stage.) Yes, if we place it here like this. Let's see . . . what else? I've got it. (He goes to the trunk and pulls out a vine or garland which he places on stage next to the ladder. He hooks a wire to it which runs up the ladder and offstage so that the vine can "grow" later in the play.) That does it . . . now we've got our beanstalk . . . and it can grow.

CLOWNS (general reaction). Great! Yes, good idea. Very good! (Etc.) (MOXY, DOXY and BOFFO bring in some additional blocks and props as needed and place them on stage.)

MUSTARD. Good! Now we're ready. Introduce the show, Boffo.

BOFFO (uncertain, but going ahead). Ladies and gentlemen! Young people of all ages! The – (Name of group.) – theatre is pleased to present an exciting new version of that age-old tale *Jack and the Beanstalk* featuring a troupe of actors from – (Town name.) – known as the . . . known as the . . . (MUSTARD goes to BOFFO and whispers in his ear.) That troupe of actors known as – The Clowns! (Fanfare. CLOWNS run together C stage and do a company pose. They break and get into place for the beginning of the story as MUSTARD opens the book and begins reading.)

MUSTARD. "Once upon a time there was a poor old woman." (As MUSTARD begins reading MOXY, DOXY and SCRAPPY prepare to play the scene. They go to the trunk and pick out their costumes, put them on and go to their places. SCRAPPY puts on cap and jacket; MOXY an apron; DOXY a rope and cowbell around her neck.

CLOWNS' PLAY

MOXY also gets bucket that was used previously for the confetti business. DOXY moves to the opposite side of the stage from MOXY and SCRAPPY.) "She had a son named Jack. She had a cow named Bessie. And that was all she had. For they were very poor and they depended for their livelihood on Old Bessie. Each morning Jack's mother sent him out with the same instructions . . . "

MOXY (playing the mother). Jack, go out and fetch the milk from Old Bessie. Take it to the marketplace, sell the milk and bring home the money. (She gives the bucket to SCRAPPY.)

SCRAPPY (playing Jack). Yes, mother, but each day Bessie seems to be giving less and less milk. And the man in the marketplace gives me fewer and fewer coins.

MOXY. I know, son. Bessie is very old. She will not give milk much longer. Treat her gently and with kindness. She's the only support we have.

SCRAPPY. Yes, mother. (He takes the bucket and moves to DOXY.) Morning, Bessie, old girl.

DOXY (playing Bessie). Morning, Jack. (The other CLOWNS react immediately to a cow speaking. BOFFO is especially outraged.)

BOFFO. Wait a minute! What is this, Doxy? Cows don't talk! What're you trying to do, make your part bigger?

DOXY (herself again). Now just a minute! I thought it was up to me to create this character. I'm *improvising*!

BOFFO. But cows don't speak!

DOXY. How do you know? Maybe you just don't understand their language.

MUSTARD (intervening). Doxy's right, Boffo. Besides, in plays it is important for us to know something about the characters — how they feel, what they're thinking, why they're doing something. So, if the character is like the cow and we don't understand her language we let her speak like the rest of us. It's called . . . um . . . um . . .

RUFFINA. Dramatic license!

BOFFO. Dramatic license?

MUSTARD. Yes, that's it. Bessie's an important character in this play. The only way we'll get to know her well is for her to speak.

BOFFO (not convinced). Ugh!

MUSTARD. So, go ahead, Doxy. You have a *license* to speak in this play.

DOXY. All right. Now, no more interruptions. (She glares at BOFFO and then returns to the character of Bessie.) Morning, Jack.

SCRAPPY (returning to character of Jack). Time for milking, Bessie. (He puts down bucket and gets block to serve as milking stool. DOXY becomes Bessie through suggestion of cow-like walk, movements and voice. [Cow-like eyelashes and/or a tail may also be added but are not absolutely necessary. There should be no attempt at reality.] She leans forward slightly so that the cowbell hangs from her neck. SCRAPPY mimes the milking business slightly behind and to one side of DOXY so that both can relate directly to the audience. It is important that the audience be part of and necessary to the action of the scene. They are, in fact, helping SCRAPPY milk the cow.) Good old girl. (He begins milking.) How come you don't give as much milk as you used to, Bessie? Aren't you feeling well?

DOXY. It isn't that, Jack. When cows get old they just don't produce milk like they did when they were younger. Someday I won't produce any more milk and you'll have to get rid of me.

SCRAPPY. No, Bessie, we couldn't get rid of you. You're one of the family.

DOXY. You'd have to, Jack. Your ma depends on this milk to live.

SCRAPPY. I know. But isn't there anything that will help?

CLOWNS' PLAY   Page 15

DOXY. Well, Jack, cows don't like to be alone. They like the sound of other cows around them. If I could just hear the sound of my friends and relatives, I wouldn't be so lonely and I might be able to produce more milk.

SCRAPPY. Bessie, I've got an idea. Let's ask our friends out there to help us. (To audience.) I bet you could all make the soothing sound of the herd. Will you, friends? Will you moo for us? Show them, Bessie . . .

DOXY. Moo . . . moo . . . moo . . . (Other CLOWNS move through audience getting the audience to follow Doxy's mooing. As the sound builds, SCRAPPY continues milking with obviously improving results.)

SCRAPPY (excited). Bessie! It's working. It's working. (He finishes and gets up.) Thank you, Bessie. (To audience.) Thank you, friends. (Rushing to MOXY.) Mother, look, Bessie has given us a full pail of milk!

MUSTARD (reading again). "And so Jack went off to the marketplace to sell his full pail of milk. He received the most money he had gotten for Bessie's milk in some time." (MUSTARD puts on farmer's hat and takes on role of Farmer Brown. He gives SCRAPPY a small bag of money. SCRAPPY runs off and MUSTARD turns to audience to continue the story.) "And this continued for several months with friends like you in the audience providing the soothing "moo" sound of the dairy herd to make Bessie a very happy cow. But then one day . . . " (SCRAPPY has returned to the milking, urging the audience to help.)

SCRAPPY. Come on, everybody! Moo . . . moo . . . moo . . . (It is obviously not working and SCRAPPY gives up.) Oh, dear, it isn't working any more. Bessie, what are we going to do?

DOXY (still playing Bessie). Poor Jack. Don't feel bad. (MOXY, playing Mother, and MUSTARD, playing Farmer Brown, go to SCRAPPY.)

MOXY. Jack, here is old Farmer Brown who always buys

our milk. Do we have any for him today?

SCRAPPY. No, Mother, Bessie cannot produce milk any more.

MOXY (to DOXY). Bessie, old girl, it looks like we'll have to sell you. You are our only livelihood.

SCRAPPY. But, Mother, if we sell her, someone will send her to the butcher for food! We must keep her! Please don't sell her!

MOXY. Jack, we have no choice. There is no other way out.

MUSTARD. Perhaps I have a solution.

MOXY. What's that, Farmer Brown?

MUSTARD. I have a small young herd that needs the guidance of a good old cow to watch over them and show them the ropes. Bessie would be perfect. And she'd always be there for you to visit, Jack. What do you say? Let me buy her from you. (SCRAPPY and MOXY are elated.)

SCRAPPY. Oh, thank you, Farmer Brown, thank you! That would be wonderful. (To DOXY.) What do you say, old girl?

DOXY (warmly). Moo!

MOXY. Thank you, Farmer Brown. It's very good of you.

MUSTARD. Well, it's all settled. Jack, you bring her over to my place tomorrow. Good day, everyone. (MUSTARD moves back to book, removes hat and returns to his role as narrator.)

MOXY. Good day, Farmer Brown.

SCRAPPY. See you tomorrow, sir.

DOXY. Moo . . . moo . . . moo

MUSTARD (reading again). "The next day Jack set out very early in the morning to deliver Bessie to Farmer Brown's pasture . . ." (SCRAPPY puts rope around Doxy's neck. They move across the stage on the road to Farmer Brown's. The sound of a circus band or calliope is heard. SCRAPPY and DOXY mime their reactions to the following action. MUSTARD puts aside his book and speaks directly to the

CLOWNS' PLAY   Page 17

audience.) What's that sound? (The other CLOWNS march in as a circus parade. As they move across the stage they mime certain circus acts and MUSTARD asks the audience to guess what they are. These should be improvised by actors according to their own abilities and interests. One might be a tightrope walker; another a trained elephant; still another a fire eater; etc. etc.) A circus parade! Let's see if you can guess what each act is. (First act.) Yes, that's it, good. (Second act.) What do you think? You sure? Of course, that's right. (Third act.) Oh, no trouble with that one. (The above lines are simply suggestions. The audience response should direct Mustard's response. The parade passes by and CLOWNS go off. MUSTARD moves back to the book.)

SCRAPPY. Gee, Bessie, that was some parade. I'd really like to go to that circus.

DOXY. Jack, now don't you disobey your mother. Remember, we're to go to Farmer Brown's place. Your mother is waiting for the money.

SCRAPPY. Oh, Bessie, come on. Let's follow them. It can't hurt anything just to watch.

(SCRAPPY pulls DOXY along toward the circus. BOFFO and TRINKET enter as two con artists from the circus. They hide behind a block or the trunk as SCRAPPY and DOXY pass by.)

BOFFO (obvious carney type). Hey, did you see that? Did you . . . did you . . . did you . . . (His mouth is watering.)

TRINKET. What are you talking about? Did I see what?

BOFFO. That kid . . . that kid was talking to the cow and . . . and . . . more important . . . The cow was talking back to the kid!

TRINKET (mocking). Kid talking to a cow . . . cow talking to a kid . . . ah, you're bananas!

BOFFO. No, I saw it. That cow talked to that kid. Come on, let's run ahead and I'll show you. (They run and hide again as SCRAPPY and DOXY pass by. DOXY tries to warn SCRAPPY by pulling back and refusing to move.)

DOXY. Jack! Jack! Don't go any further. You must take me to Farmer Brown's. Your mother is counting on you.

SCRAPPY (ignoring her). Come on, Bessie. It's just for a little while. I've just got to see that circus. (They move off. BOFFO and TRINKET emerge from their hiding place.)

BOFFO. Now do you believe me?

TRINKET (stunned). I can't believe my ears.

BOFFO. Look, we've got to get our hands on that cow. We'd have it made with the circus. There's not another act like that in the whole world.

TRINKET. And just how do you propose to heist that heifer?

BOFFO (confused). Heist the heifer? Heist the heifer? (He bops TRINKET on the head. She falls to the floor.) Oh, that's cute. What does that mean?

TRINKET (mad). Steal the cow!

BOFFO. Shh! You crazy? Someone will hear you.

TRINKET (whispering). Well, how are you going to capture the cow?

BOFFO. Simple.

TRINKET. What?

BOFFO. Simp – lif – ic – o!

TRINKET. Well, I'd like to know how!

BOFFO. We are not going to steal the cow at all. We are going to buy her!

TRINKET. You've wrenched your noggin.

BOFFO. What?

TRINKET. You've fractured your frisbee.

BOFFO. Huh? I don't understand?

TRINKET. You've blown your bandanna. (BOFFO now ignores her. He thinks.)

CLOWNS' PLAY   Page 19

BOFFO. Now listen. Let's give the kid the old magic bean bit.
TRINKET. What?
BOFFO. You know, the old magic bean bit.
TRINKET. You mean, those beans you got from that old guy on the road last week? (Laughing.) The ones he told you that if you planted they'd grow to the sky? (She can hardly contain herself.) Boy, did you get taken!
BOFFO. Maybe not. (Takes beans from pocket.) These beans are going to get us that talking cow. They're going to make us rich! Come on. (They run off.)

(SCRAPPY returns, pulling DOXY.)

SCRAPPY. Come on, Bessie. I just want to see a little bit of the circus.
DOXY (resisting). No, Jack, no!

(BOFFO and TRINKET intercept SCRAPPY and DOXY.)

BOFFO. Psst! Psst! Hey, kid, what's the matter?
SCRAPPY. I want to go to the circus and my cow doesn't, mister.
BOFFO. Look, kid, you shouldn't let a cow tell you what to do.
DOXY (trying to pull SCRAPPY away). Moo! Moo!
BOFFO. So, you want to see the circus?
SCRAPPY. Oh, yes, sir, very much. I've never been to a real circus. But my mother told me to take old Bessie here to Farmer Brown's place. Bessie can't give milk any more and Farmer Brown is going to buy her from us.
DOXY (as before) Moo! Moo!
BOFFO (looking over DOXY like a used car). Can't give milk any more, huh?
SCRAPPY. No, sir.

TRINKET (echoing BOFFO). Not much good on the farm any more ...

DOXY. Moo! Moo!

BOFFO. Good for nothing but chewing her cud!

DOXY. Moo! Moo!

TRINKET (setting SCRAPPY up for the con). Certainly not worth anything ... but ...

SCRAPPY. Farmer Brown says he'll pay money so that Bessie can teach the young cows in his herd.

BOFFO. Of course, old Bessie's not worth anything ... but ...

DOXY. Moo! Moo!

SCRAPPY. But what? (BOFFO pulls TRINKET aside to tweak Scrappy's curiosity.)

BOFFO. Should we tell him?

TRINKET. Well, I'm not so sure ... um ...

BOFFO. Look, he's a nice-looking kid. And, well, he's really got a yen to go to the circus.

TRINKET. Yeah, but that's a pretty bad-tempered cow!

DOXY. Moo! Moo! Moo!

BOFFO. Certainly is. But, what the heck!

TRINKET. Yeah, what the heck!

SCRAPPY (curious). What do you mean — what the heck?

DOXY. Moo! Moo!

BOFFO. Come here, kid. (SCRAPPY hesitates.) It's okay. Let my friend here hold the cow. (TRINKET takes the rope cautiously. BOFFO takes SCRAPPY aside.) Tell you what I'm going to do, kid.

SCRAPPY. Yes?

DOXY. Moo! Moo! (TRINKET tries to quiet her.)

BOFFO. I supposed you've guessed that my friend and I are clowns with the circus. It just so happens we've been looking for a cow to put in our act for some time.

DOXY. Moo! Moo!

BOFFO. Now along you come with a cow. It's our good

CLOWNS' PLAY

fortune. Even if she is a bit over-the-hill . . .

DOXY. Moo! Moo!

BOFFO (ignoring her). We'd like to buy her from you.

SCRAPPY. Gee, you would?

DOXY. Moo! Moo!

BOFFO. Of course, I couldn't pay money like Farmer Brown, but I have something better than money.

SCRAPPY (not so sure). Better than money?

BOFFO. Yeah. Look. Tickets to the circus and . . . these.

SCRAPPY. What are they?

BOFFO. Beans!

SCRAPPY. Beans?

BOFFO and TRINKET (together). Magic beans!

SCRAPPY. Magic beans?

DOXY. Moo! Moo!

BOFFO. Well, what do you say, kid?

SCRAPPY. Gee, mister, I'd sure like to go to the circus but . . . what could we do with the beans?

BOFFO. Kid, these aren't ordinary magic beans like you can buy at any carnival. These are *real* magic beans like in . . . fairy tales! They were given to me by a gypsy who told me . . . (Imitating gypsy.) "Take these magic beans. They are for the young at heart. And if you plant these beans in the ground at sundown, they will grow to the sky by sunrise."

SCRAPPY (stunned). Gee . . .

DOXY (sensing she is losing). Moo! Moo!

SCRAPPY. Oh, but I can't. I can't sell Bessie for circus tickets and magic beans. My mother would . . .

BOFFO. Kid, look . . . I'll give you a guarantee!

SCRAPPY. A what?

BOFFO. A guarantee. I'll just put it in writing. (He takes out an over-sized pencil and long scroll which he unravels across stage.) If these magic beans don't do what I say . . . (He writes.) If these magic beans do not grow to the sky

and bring you good fortune, I will guarantee that I will give you back your cow!
SCRAPPY. Gee, that's pretty fair, mister.
BOFFO. Well, what do you say? Do we have a deal?
TRINKET. Yeah, what do you say?
DOXY (resigned). Moo!
SCRAPPY. All right. I'll do it.
BOFFO (moving in quickly). Here's your tickets, kid. And here's your beans.
TRINKET. Now, we'll just take this cow off to the circus. (She starts out with DOXY.)
SCRAPPY. Wait a minute! Could I just have a minute to say good-bye to Old Bessie?
BOFFO. Sure . . . let the kid say good-bye to his cow. (He beckons TRINKET away.)
SCRAPPY (to DOXY). Good-bye, old girl. I'll come to the circus and see you.
DOXY (whispering). Jack, change your mind. It's not too late. Those people are con artists. Don't trust them!
BOFFO (breaking in). Okay, time's up. We've got to be going.
SCRAPPY. Good-bye, Bessie. (To audience.) Friends, let's say good-bye together to Old Bessie. (BOFFO and TRINKET start out, pulling DOXY along after them.) All right, together now — Good-bye, Old Bessie! Wave to her. Again — Good-bye, Old Bessie! Boy, I'm sure going to miss her. But, now I'm off to the circus! (He runs off.)
MUSTARD (reading again). "And so, Jack went to the circus. He spent the whole day there until it was dark outside. He saw all the acts and then went back and met all the performers. He had a glorious day! But when the circus was over . . ."

(SCRAPPY returns to the stage and mimes the walk home. Using the traditional "walking-in-place" mime he shows us

CLOWNS' PLAY

Jack walking home after the circus and his reactions to the environmental sounds and lighting which MUSTARD calls for as he describes the journey home.) "It was very late and very dark out. Jack's mother was surely worried about him. And, a storm was brewing in the sky." (He breaks from his reading to directly address the audience.) Now we'll need your help to tell this part of the story — Jack's journey home in the dark of night and in the midst of a fearsome storm. We can do the thunder sound easily. (A CLOWN brings out a thunder sheet and shakes it for thunder sound.) And with the help of the lighting person — (Signals and we get lightning effect.) Lightning! Ah, the magic of the theatre! But our wind machine is broken and we're going to need some help to make the wind sound that we need for this scene. Let's hear your wind sound. (Other CLOWNS help until the audience gets it.) Oh, that's good. Now, watch for the wind sign. (A CLOWN has "wind" sign; another CLOWN a "thunder" sign and another CLOWN a "lightning" sign.) That's your cue to make the sound. Okay, are we ready? (They will say yes.) Now, we're ready to continue . . . (He returns to reading the story.) "It was very late and very dark out. Jack's mother was surely worried about him. And, a storm was brewing in the sky. (SCRAPPY has picked up mime again.) Jack moved quickly through the dark countryside. His eyes searched the black environment around him in fear of what might be lurking in the bushes, rocks and trees around him . . . ("Wind." MUSTARD continues reading over sounds and lighting effects. The whole effect should be a kind of orchestration of mood with the reading, the mime, the sounds, and the lighting all playing their part.) Small objects darted in front of him. They were most probably rabbits or squirrels, but in Jack's mind they seemed to be the ferocious lions and tigers he had seen at the circus — and he was afraid . . .

("Lightning" and "Thunder.") He made believe for a moment that he was the lion-tamer at the circus — fearless and brave — (SCRAPPY mimes lion-tamer.) — moving the animals back, back, back until they knew he was their master. But a large clap of thunder . . . ("Thunder.") . . . reminded him that he must hurry home. His mother would be worried. And, besides, he wanted to show her the magic beans. The wind . . . ("Wind.") . . . whisked him along the road and soon he could see his mother off in the distance . . . (MOXY mimes mother's actions.) . . . looking out of her window. She was terribly worried. And the storm was beginning to rage." ("Wind," "Lightning," "Thunder." After a long final stormy moment, MUSTARD cuts it off like an orchestra conductor and then turns to the audience.) Thank you for helping me make this transition from one part of the story to the other. (He signals to SCRAPPY and MOXY to begin playing the next scene.)

MOXY. Jack, where have you been? I have been worried sick!

SCRAPPY. Mother, I must tell you what happened. I met a man from the circus and he gave me tickets.

MOXY. That's wonderful, Jack. But did you get Old Bessie to Farmer Brown's?

SCRAPPY (hesitant). Well, not exactly.

MOXY. What do you mean — not exactly?

SCRAPPY. Well, we did start out for Farmer Brown's, but we . . . we ran into a circus parade and . . .

MOXY (skeptical). Yes?

SCRAPPY. Oh, Mother, it was wonderful. I've never seen anything like it. They had lions and tigers, bareback riders, elephants and clowns, and, and . . .

MOXY. Jack! Tell me what happened to Old Bessie.

SCRAPPY. Well, as I told you . . . I met this man on the way to Farmer Brown's. He and his friend were clowns with the circus. He gave me tickets to the circus and . . . and . . .

CLOWNS' PLAY

(Blurts it out.) He bought Old Bessie from me!

MOXY. Bought Bessie from you?

SCRAPPY. Yes, Mother. He said that they wanted her . . .

MOXY (cutting him off). Well, that's okay. Farmer Brown will be disappointed but as long as you got the money. How much did he give you?

SCRAPPY. I . . . I . . .

MOXY. Jack! You did get money for Old Bessie?

SCRAPPY. Not exactly . . .

MOXY. Jack!

SCRAPPY (quickly). I got something better than money! I got . . .

MOXY (stunned). Something better than money?

SCRAPPY. Yes. Yes. (He pulls beans from pocket.) Look. These are genuine fairy tale magic beans!

MOXY (incredulous). Genuine fairy tale magic beans?

SCRAPPY (proud). And I got a guarantee, too. (He pulls the "guarantee" out and unrolls it.)

MOXY. Guarantee?

SCRAPPY. Yes. If the beans don't grow to the sky and provide good fortune to us, we will get Bessie back.

MOXY (too upset to be mad). Oh, Jack . . . Jack . . . Oh! I should punish you. But having no cow *and* no money will be punishment enough.

SCRAPPY. But, Mother, the man promised me they'd grow and give us good fortune.

MOXY. Don't you see, son? You've been taken in. That clown was a con man. He just wanted to cheat you out of your cow, though heaven knows why he would want Old Bessie.

SCRAPPY. You mean, the beans won't grow to the sky?

MOXY. I'm afraid not.

SCRAPPY. You mean, we won't find good fortune?

MOXY. Only in our dreams, Jack.

SCRAPPY (mad). Well, he can't do that to me! I'm going

back and demand he give Bessie back to me!
MOXY. No, Jack — calm down. You can be certain that the con man is long gone from here by now. Besides, the storm is too bad for traveling.
SCRAPPY. Oh, Mother, I'm so sorry!
MOXY. Maybe you've learned a lesson from this, son. Now, go get yourself ready for bed and I'll fix you a bit of food. It's the last we have but we'll worry about that tomorrow.
SCRAPPY. Oh, Mother, I'm . . .
MOXY. Never mind. Go get ready for bed. (SCRAPPY starts to go, then hesitates.)
SCRAPPY. But what about the beans? (A thought.) Maybe we should plant them, just to see if . . .
MOXY (exasperated). Jack! Haven't you learned? I'll show you what to do with these beans. (She throws them out an imaginary window.) Now, get ready for bed.
SCRAPPY. Yes, Mother. (He goes. The stage is now in complete darkness except for a spot where Moxy has thrown the beans at the base of the ladder. Mustard's voice is heard from the darkness reading.)
MUSTARD. "That night as the storm pounded against the house, Jack could not sleep . . . (Light up on SCRAPPY.) He thought about the events of the day — the con man, the circus, Bessie, and those supposedly genuine fairy tale magic beans. He peered out through the storm at the place where his mother had thrown those beans and he wished and wished something would happen."
SCRAPPY. Beans, you've got to grow! You've just got to! My Mother and I need help. I did a dumb thing today. You've just got to grow! (To audience.) Friends, will you help me wish? Maybe if we wished together — like when you helped me milk Old Bessie — maybe if we wished hard enough together, the beans would grow. Will you help me? (They will say yes.) All right then — wish hard! Grow! Grow! Keep it up. Grow! Grow! Grow! (At

CLOWNS' PLAY

this point the vine starts "climbing" the ladder.) Friends, it's working. It's working! Keep it up. Grow! Grow! Grow! (They keep it up until the vine has disappeared in the flies.) It worked! It worked! Thank you, friends, for your good wishes. (Lights up.) It's morning. I must tell my Mother. (Calling.) Mother! Mother! Wake up!

MOXY (bleary). What is it, Jack, what is it?

SCRAPPY. Look!

MOXY. Well, I'll be . . .

SCRAPPY. Mother, I wished and wished as hard as I could. And with the help of my friends out there . . . (Indicates audience.) . . . the beans grew to the sky!

MOXY (to audience). Oh, thank you for helping my boy. Thank you.

SCRAPPY. Mother, I've got to climb the vine to the top. The con man said that I would find good fortune there. (Thinking.) Mother, maybe he wasn't a con man after all.

MOXY. Yes, maybe you're right. (SCRAPPY runs to the vine and starts to "climb." MOXY follows.) Be careful now, son. Keep a good footing. And be very careful when you get to the top. No telling what you may find up there.

SCRAPPY. I'll be careful. Wish me luck.

MOXY. Good luck, son!

MUSTARD (reading again). "Jack climbed and climbed — and then he climbed some more . . ."

SCRAPPY (resting on vine). Phew! This is hard work. It seems like I'll never get to the top.

MUSTARD (reading). "But he continued to climb and climb and climb and climb and climb until he poked his head through the clouds and reached the top. (During this SCRAPPY has "disappeared" up the ladder and down the other side out of sight of the audience.) At the top, he saw a strange winding road which seemed to go on and on."

(SCRAPPY enters from the wings and mimes the actions of running and walking down the road in this strange land.)

MUSTARD (reading). "He ran at first but then realized that he must walk to conserve his energy. He walked and walked down that road until his feet hurt terribly with every step he took. Finally, he came upon a big house. It was huge and he marveled at its size. At first, he hesitated, but ..."

SCRAPPY (gathering his courage). What's the matter with me? This is what I came for. (He goes to imaginary door and knocks.) Maybe I'll find good fortune here.

(RUFFINA enters as the Giant's wife.)

RUFFINA. What's this? What are you doing here?
SCRAPPY. Good morning. I'm looking for good fortune!
RUFFINA. Good fortune, huh? Do you know where you are?
SCRAPPY. No, ma'am.
RUFFINA. Well, I'll tell you. This is the land of the Giant.
SCRAPPY (gulping). The Giant?
RUFFINA. Yes, the Giant — I'm his wife. And I'll tell you, boy — he likes to eat boys like you for breakfast. Yes, sir, fresh boys on toast with strawberry jam!
SCRAPPY. He does?
RUFFINA (beginning to like him). Ah, but don't be afraid. He's big and gruff and strong, and he appears quite ferocious, but he's a real pussy cat inside!
SCRAPPY. He is?
RUFFINA. Sure. Don't worry. I can handle the big ox!
MUSCULO (offstage, growling as Giant). Wife. Wife. Where are you, wife? I want my breakfast. Wife. Wife.
RUFFINA. Quick, hide yourself! (She opens top of a large block for SCRAPPY to hide in. He climbs in and she shuts

CLOWNS' PLAY   Page 29

it.) Hide yourself until I quiet him down a bit.

(MUSCULO, as Giant, enters.)

MUSCULO. Oh, there you are. I've been looking all over for you. I've been thump-thumping through the thicket. (He smells something in the air.) Wait! What is it? My nose tells me . . . (Sniffing.)

RUFFINA (sweetly). Yes, husband?

MUSCULO (begins Giant routine but can't remember). Ah? Bum-Boom . . . Zam . . . ah . . . Koo . . . Sing . . . ah . . . Ah bilg! (Breaking character.) Oh, phooey! I can't remember!

MUSTARD (reacting with other CLOWNS). What is it? What's the matter, Musculo?

MUSCULO. I can't remember the lines!

BOFFO. But, Musculo, you're improvising. You can make it up as you go along.

MUSCULO. You dunce! These are some of the most famous lines in the whole story. I've got to get them just right. These people out there expect me to at least get the main things into the story. We owe it to them.

MUSTARD. You're right, Musculo. Come over here and look at the book. (MUSCULO crosses to MUSTARD.) See. Here it is — "Fee Fi Fo Fum, I Smell the Blood of An Englishman, Be He Alive or Be He Dead, I'll Grind His Bones To Make My Bread." (MUSTARD reads this like a frustrated actor.)

MUSCULO. Yes, that's it. Let me try — Fee Fum Fo Fi . . .

MUSTARD. No! No! Fee Fi Fo Fum.

MUSCULO. That's right — Fee Fi Fo Fum. (He says it carefully, relieved that he's got it.) I smell the blood of an Englishman, be he . . . ah . . . be he . . . Oh, drat! I'll never remember! (The other CLOWNS are getting upset with him. MUSTARD steps in. SCRAPPY comes out of box.)

MUSTARD. Wait! I've got an idea, Musculo. I'll just tear this page from the book . . . (He tears out page which is really a large cue card.) . . . and I'll put it up on this easel. (The easel holds the "Show Today" sign.) And when you get to the times that you have to say the Giant's verse, we'll get our friends in the audience to do it for you. (He is pleased with himself.)

MUSCULO. Gee, that would be great. (To audience.) Can you do it, audience? (They will say yes.)

MUSTARD. Of course they can. They know the story better than we do. Come on now, back to the play. (Everyone returns to original place for playing the scene.)

MUSCULO. Okay. Let's take it from my entrance, Ruffina. Give me my cue . . . (He exits.)

RUFFINA. Okay. (She returns to role of Giant's wife.) Don't worry, I can handle the big ox.

MUSCULO (offstage). Wife. Wife. Where are you? I want my breakfast.

RUFFINA. Quick, hide yourself until I have a chance to quiet him down. (SCRAPPY hides again.)

(MUSCULO enters.)

MUSCULO. There you are. I've been looking all over for you. Wait. What is that smell? (Sniffing.)

RUFFINA. Smell, husband? (MUSCULO signals to MUSTARD that he is ready for the verse. MUSTARD goes to cue card and leads audience.) Yes . . . smell! Ah . . . Fee Fi Fo Fum, I smell the blood of an Englishman, be he alive or be he dead, I'll grind his bones to make my bread . . . (To audience, out of character.) Thanks. (Back to character.) Where is he?

RUFFINA. Who, dear? I don't smell anything.

MUSCULO. You don't?

RUFFINA. No. Nothing. Except the fragrance of the flowers

CLOWNS' PLAY   Page 31

from the meadow.

MUSCULO. Flowers from the meadow?

RUFFINA. Yes. (She grabs flowers from the trunk.) These! (Hands MUSCULO a bouquet.)

MUSCULO (sniffing flowers). Funny, I've never known the flowers from the meadow to smell like a little boy. I so love little boys on toast with . . . oh, dear . . . (He's hungry.) . . . with strawberry jam!

RUFFINA. I know you do, dear. Maybe you'll find a tasty young boy soon. Sit down. I'll fix you a nice breakfast. (MUSCULO sits on block in which SCRAPPY is hiding.) Ah . . . wouldn't you like to sit over here, dear?

MUSCULO. No! You know this is my favorite place to sit.

RUFFINA. But, pussy cat!

MUSCULO. Now, don't pussy cat me! Get my gold for counting! And get my breakfast!

RUFFINA. Yes, dear. (She starts out, hesitates.) You *sure* you wouldn't rather sit over here, dear?

MUSCULO. I told you no! Get my gold and my breakfast! (RUFFINA exits.) Hmm? (Sniffing.) I still smell something. (He signals MUSTARD for same verse business as before. MUSTARD leads audience and MUSCULO follows along.) Fee Fi Fo Fum, I smell the blood of an Englishman. (He moves away from the block. SCRAPPY gets about halfway out of the box when MUSCULO turns back. SCRAPPY ducks back into block.) Be he alive or be he dead, I'll grind his bones to make my bread. (He sits back on the block.)

(RUFFINA returns.)

RUFFINA. Here's your bag of gold, dear. (She leaves it on the other side of the stage so that he will have to get up to get it. She quickly exits.)

MUSCULO. What's got into that woman? (He gets up

grumpily to get the bag.)

(As MUSCULO moves to the bag, RUFFINA sneaks in from another direction, goes to Scrappy's block, opens it and whispers inside to him.)

RUFFINA (whispering). Boy, are you okay? Sit tight. I'll get you out soon. (As MUSCULO turns to go back to his seat, RUFFINA goes off quickly. MUSCULO does not see her.)

MUSCULO (sitting on block). Ah, my gold! I love to count my gold. Hmm? That smell again. Oh, no matter. (He counts.) One. Two. Three. Four. Five. (He is getting sleepy.) I'm getting very sleepy . . . very sleepy. Must have thumped through the thicket just too much this morning. (He yawns.) That smell! Six . . . Seven . . . (He falls asleep, head hanging, but he is still very much on the block.)

(RUFFINA enters. She is immediately faced with the problem of getting MUSCULO off the block so that she can get SCRAPPY out of it.)

RUFFINA. Let's see. How am I going to get that big lug off that block and get the boy out? (She thinks for a moment.) I've got it! (She proceeds to fold MUSCULO up — head, arms, legs — making him as compact as possible but with him still on the block. She thinks again for a moment, gets an idea. She runs off into the wings and returns immediately with a wheelbarrow and moves it next to the block so that she can simply roll MUSCULO off the block and into the wheelbarrow. She does this with great precision.) There! (She dusts off her hands.) You big lug! (She leaves him sleeping peacefully in the wheelbarrow and goes to the block and opens it.) Come

CLOWNS' PLAY

out, boy. It's all right now. (SCRAPPY emerges from the block.) Look now, you'd better go before he wakes up and . . . (She wants to give him something.) . . . here, take this with you. (She picks up a bag of gold and gives it to SCRAPPY.) We have plenty. Maybe it will give you the good fortune you seek.

SCRAPPY. Oh, thank you, ma'am! (He starts to go, then stops.) But, must you stay here? Why don't you climb down the beanstalk with me? You could live with my mother and me.

RUFFINA. No, boy, I must watch out for my husband, the Giant. He's not a bad person. He's just been gianting so long he doesn't know any other way to behave. I'll be okay. This is my home. Good-bye.

SCRAPPY. Good-bye. (He goes off.)

MUSCULO (waking). Hmm! I must have snoozed. (Notices he is in wheelbarrow.) What am I doing in this thing? (He reaches for bag of gold.) Where's my gold? My gold!

RUFFINA. Dear, you did doze off. And while you were sleeping, I . . . (Thinking quickly.) I bought this new kind of bed for you!

MUSCULO. A whole bag of gold for this?

RUFFINA. They're very expensive, dear. Everyone in Giantland is getting one.

MUSCULO (not so sure but resigned). Hmph! Well, woman, I'm still hungry. Where's my breakfast?

RUFFINA. Right away, dear — right away. (She exits.)

MUSTARD (reading). "Jack was so happy that his feet nearly flew him back to the top of the beanstalk . . ."

(SCRAPPY enters to one side of the stage and looks down as if at the top of the beanstalk.)

SCRAPPY. Gee, this bag is heavy! How am I going to get it down the beanstalk? It's such a long climb. I know. I'll drop it down. (He drops bag into trap or off the front of the stage out of view of the audience.) Look out below!

(The lights go out on SCRAPPY as he starts to climb down. They immediately come up on the ladder and a moment later we see the bag of gold drop to the ground. MOXY enters as Jack's Mother again.)

MOXY. Jack, Jack, is that you? (She sees the bag of gold.) What's this? Gold? Gold? (She looks up vine.) Jack, are you all right? Son, are you all right? (SCRAPPY appears at the top of the ladder and begins climbing down.)
SCRAPPY. Mother, I'm fine — I'm fine. Did you see what I brought home?
MOXY. Yes, son, but where did you get it?
SCRAPPY. Oh, Mother, there was a very nice lady — the wife of the Giant of Giantland and when I got there . . .
MUSTARD (picks up reading again). "And Jack told his mother the whole story of his adventures at the top of the beanstalk — how he had received good fortune. And Jack and his mother grew prosperous thanks to the gold which the kind wife of the Giant had given him. Meanwhile, back in Giantland . . ."

(MUSCULO enters.)

MUSCULO. Fee Fi . . . Oh, fiddle faddle! I don't smell anything! I'm so tired of steaks and chops and cheese and vegetables. I need a good choice juicy . . . (To audience in character.) Oh, you all look so good to me! I could . . .

(MUSCULO starts to go into the audience when RUFFINA enters.)

RUFFINA. Husband! Come here and sit down. (MUSCULO

CLOWNS' PLAY

does so.) Husband, you are getting mighty testy lately! Maybe it's time for you to retire.

MUSCULO. Retire?

RUFFINA. Yes. You've been gianting too long. You used to be a nice giant but lately you are getting very nasty.

MUSCULO. Nasty?

RUFFINA. Yes, nasty!

MUSCULO. Now look here, woman! Quit bugging me! I like being a giant. It's fun being bigger and stronger and more powerful and smarter . . .

RUFFINA. Smarter? (She starts to laugh, thinks better of it.)

MUSCULO. Now, go in and get my golden hen.

RUFFINA. What, again? We've got enough golden eggs. We certainly don't need any more.

MUSCULO. I want more! Now go on and get my hen! (A disturbance is heard in the wings. MUSCULO and RUFFINA break character.) What's that?

(BOFFO is pulled on stage by DOXY and TRINKET. They are being themselves.)

BOFFO. I'm not going to do it! No way! There are some things you just can't ask me to do!

TRINKET. But Mustard is the director and says that . . .

DOXY. If I can play a cow, you can play a hen — you old goat!

MUSTARD. Boffo, are you causing trouble again?

BOFFO. I'm not going to do it. I'm not going to play a hen — cluck clucking all over the place. It's demeaning. It's not respectable for a clown of my stature. (MUSTARD is not perturbed.)

MUSTARD. All right then, I'll do it. I'll play the hen!

CLOWNS (general reaction). You?

MUSTARD. Why not? I think I would make an excellent hen. You just wait and see. (He starts off.) Continue!
MUSCULO (picking up where he left off). Go on, wife — get the hen. (RUFFINA goes. MUSCULO turns to the audience and speaks to them as Giant.) You see, I have this very special golden hen who lays golden eggs. Not eggs you eat, but solid gold! Each one is worth more than a whole bag of gold. No one knows the secret of getting the hen to lay the golden eggs except me. Not even my wife knows.

(RUFFINA returns, pulling MUSTARD behind as a hen. MUSTARD plays the hen through movement and mime. He proudly waddles and struts around the stage. He has on a brightly-colored coat with tails under which the eggs can be hidden.)

RUFFINA. Here's your hen. All you can think of is eating little boys and girls and getting this hen to lay golden eggs. We have enough! Let's retire and give up the life of a giant.
MUSCULO. Retire? Not as long as I have my golden hen. (Gives MUSTARD a pat.) Begone, woman! (RUFFINA goes. MUSCULO calls after her.) And bring in my singing harp to soothe my mood. Come here, hen. (MUSTARD waddles over.)
MUSTARD (as hen). Cluck. Cluck. Cluck.
MUSCULO. Ah, you're a good hen. Never give me any trouble. Just lay your beautiful golden eggs.
MUSTARD. Cluck. Cluck. Cluck.
MUSCULO. Now let's have one of your super-colossal eggs . . . (He cautiously gets up and looks around to see if anyone is watching.) Good. No one around. Can't be too careful. You are a very precious little hen.
MUSTARD. Cluck. Cluck. (MUSCULO reaches inside his

shirt and brings out a little pouch tied around his neck. He takes out the secret formula for egg laying.)

MUSCULO. Here it is. Now, let's see . . . (He reads formula and performs actions indicated.) Make like a hen, three times around. (Does so.) Clap your hands, stomp on the ground. (Does so.) Raise your arms, move your legs. (Does so.) Cluck once more and you'll find an egg. (Completes ritual.)

MUSTARD. Cluck. Cluck. Cluck. (Builds "clucks" until he lays an egg [which is styrofoam egg hidden in coat].)

MUSCULO (overjoyed). Oh, beautiful, beautiful . . . (He holds up the egg.)

(RUFFINA returns.)

RUFFINA. Not another egg! Oh, husband, we don't need it. Let's give away the golden hen and retire!

MUSCULO. Nonsense. I shall never retire as long as there is one egg left in that golden hen. Where's my harp?

(RUFFINA goes to get harp in wings. TRINKET portrays the harp. She has string tied from her outstretched arm to her foot. RUFFINA leads her in immediately.)

RUFFINA. Here you are. (She starts to go, then stops.) Won't you even think about giving up this giant business?

MUSCULO. Never! Now leave me alone! (RUFFINA goes.) Give up gianting . . . give up gianting . . . that woman must be crazy! (He sits, gets comfortable.) Sing, harp, sing! (TRINKET sings sweetly.) I shall never give up this life as long as I have my singing harp and my golden hen . . . (He snoozes. MUSTARD becomes the narrator again and quickly runs over to the book and reads the transition. MUSCULO goes offstage.)

MUSTARD (reading). "Not long after that, Jack ventured

up the beanstalk again to see his friend — the giant's wife."

(SCRAPPY enters cautiously. RUFFINA is miming picking flowers from the meadow. While she is bending over, SCRAPPY taps her on the shoulder, frightening her.)

SCRAPPY. Ma'am.
RUFFINA. Heavens! It's you, boy. You frightened me so!
SCRAPPY. I'm sorry. I didn't mean to frighten you.
RUFFINA. That's all right, boy. I'm afraid I was lost in thought — miles away from Giantland.
SCRAPPY. I had to come back to see how you were. And I wanted to tell you how prosperous we have become since you gave us that bag of gold. We owe it all to you.
RUFFINA. That was very thoughtful of you, boy. But you'd better turn around and go on back down that road and scamper down that beanstalk. The Giant is in a terrible temper today. He hasn't had a boy to eat in some time. He can smell you a mile away.
SCRAPPY. Oh, I'm sorry I . . .
MUSCULO (offstage). Fo Fum Fee Fi . . . Darn it!
CLOWNS (together). Not again!
MUSTARD (to audience). Come on — help him out one more time, will you? Okay . . . (He leads them.)
MUSCULO (following audience). Fee Fi Fo Fum, I smell the blood of an Englishman, be he alive or be he dead, I'll grind his bones to make my bread . . .
MUSTARD (to audience). Thanks again.
MUSCULO (offstage). Where is he?
RUFFINA. You must hide! (SCRAPPY runs to the block.) No, not there!
MUSCULO (still offstage). Where is he? I smell a delicious boy!
RUFFINA. Where shall I hide you?
MUSCULO (still offstage). I've not had a fresh boy on toast

CLOWNS' PLAY

with strawberry jam in ages!

RUFFINA (thinking quickly). I have it. (She indicates the audience.) How about out there? I'm sure they'd protect you and not tell the Giant where you are. Go on, find a seat out there. (SCRAPPY runs into the audience.)

SCRAPPY. Please hide me. (He finds a seat somewhere in the middle. He sits with a child on his lap, hiding him.)

RUFFINA (to audience). Shh! Please don't tell.

(MUSCULO enters. He looks all over the stage, sniffing. Then he turns to the audience.)

MUSCULO. Is he out there? (RUFFINA and the other CLOWNS try to help by reminding the audience.)

RUFFINA and CLOWNS. Shh! (MUSCULO continues to look out at the audience. He moves into the audience and through the front aisles.)

MUSCULO. Are you sitting on him? Is he under you? Hmm . . . maybe I'll eat one of you instead! (RUFFINA tries to distract MUSCULO. She points offstage.)

RUFFINA. There he is!

MUSCULO. Where? Ah, I'll get him. (He runs offstage.)

RUFFINA. Okay, boy . . . you can come up now. The coast is clear.

SCRAPPY (to audience as he moves to the stage). Thank you, friends. Thank you for helping me. (To RUFFINA.) Phew! That was a close call. He is in a mood.

RUFFINA. Yes. You better scurry to the beanstalk. And take my advice – never come back again.

SCRAPPY. But what about you?

RUFFINA. I'll be all right. I'm trying to get him to retire. One of these days he will . . .

MUSCULO (offstage). Fee Fi Fo Fum.

MUSTARD (to audience). He remembered!

RUFFINA (to SCRAPPY). He's coming back. Hurry! Hurry!

Run!
SCRAPPY. Good-bye and thank you!
MUSCULO (offstage). Fee Fi Fo Fum.
MUSTARD (to audience). He remembered again!
RUFFINA (stopping SCRAPPY). Wait a minute! (She goes and gets TRINKET and MUSTARD. She ties them together so that SCRAPPY can pull them along behind him.) Take these along with you.
SCRAPPY. Oh, I couldn't.
RUFFINA. Please, boy. You want to help me. This is the only way. The harp sings and the hen lays golden eggs. I don't have the secret formula for making the hen lay eggs but a boy like you, who can climb the beanstalk and keep from being the Giant's breakfast — maybe you can find out what it is. They could bring you lots of money.
SCRAPPY. But we don't need any more.
RUFFINA. Then give it to those who do. Take them, boy. And hurry!
MUSCULO (closer but still offstage). Fee Fi Fo Fum!

(MUSCULO enters down a house aisle. He carries an oversized jar in his hand. He spots SCRAPPY.)

MUSCULO. There you are! Come here, you tasty morsel. The strawberry jam is waiting. (He chases SCRAPPY with TRINKET and MUSTARD in tow through the aisles of the theatre and finally offstage.)

(MOXY, as Mother, enters to base of ladder and looks up.)

MOXY. Jack! What's going on up there? Come down here at once.
SCRAPPY (offstage). I'm coming, Mother. I'm coming. (TRINKET and MUSTARD climb down the ladder.) Take care of our new friends. (As he is coming down.) Mother,

CLOWNS' PLAY

quick, get me an ax. (MOXY runs and gets ax from trunk.) Hurry, Mother.

MOXY (handing ax to SCRAPPY). Jack, what are you going to do?

SCRAPPY. We have all the good fortune we need. I must chop down the beanstalk. (To audience.) It'll take five whacks to chop it down. Please help me. Ready? Whack! Whack! Whack! Whack! Whack! Oh, dear, not quite enough. Three more, please — ready — Whack! Whack! Whack! (The vine falls.) Timber!

MOXY. Jack, what happened up there?

SCRAPPY. I'll tell you all about it later, Mother. First, meet our new friends. This is the singing harp. Listen. (He pushes Trinket's nose to make her sing. She does.) And this is the golden hen that lays golden eggs. The Giant's wife gave them to us. I don't know how to get the hen to lay a golden egg. It takes a secret formula but the Giant's wife said I might figure it out.

MOXY. We don't need more gold, Jack.

SCRAPPY. I know, Mother. But maybe we could help others with it. (MUSTARD, as the hen, whispers in Scrappy's ear.) What? (Looking at audience.) They know it? You know it? (Some in audience may respond immediately but a member of the audience has been planted to bring up big cue card with verse on it at this time.) Oh, look — someone wrote it down. Thank you. (Audience member who brings up formula should stay to do actions with the CLOWNS.) Well, let's try it. Come on, everybody — together: Make like a hen, three times around. (CLOWNS and audience together.) Clap your hands, stomp on the ground. (Everyone again.) Raise your arms, move your legs. (Everyone again.) Cluck once more and you'll find an egg. (Everyone again.)

MUSTARD. Cluck. Cluck. Cluck. (Another egg is produced.)

SCRAPPY. Look at this wonderful egg! (Everyone applauds.)
MUSTARD (himself again). Well, that's it. The story's over. Come on, everyone — put all our props away . . .
BOFFO (upset). Wait a minute! You can't end it there. What happened to the Giant? (MUSTARD looks to MUSCULO and RUFFINA, who put their heads together to work out an improvisation.)
MUSTARD. Look! (RUFFINA sits on block sewing. She is the Giant's wife again. MUSCULO, the Giant again, is pleading with her.)
MUSCULO. How could you do this to me, wife? My wonderful hen and my beautiful harp! (Sobbing.)
RUFFINA (she is now in control). Never you mind. We're retired now. Bring me my breakfast! Fetch me my mirror! Mow the lawn! Paint the house!
MUSCULO. Yes, dear! Yes, dear! Right away, dear! Anything you say, dear! (Everyone laughs and applauds.)
MOXY. And what happened to Bessie the cow and the con man? (BOFFO, DOXY and SCRAPPY put their heads together to work it out. BOFFO becomes the con man again. He leads DOXY, as Bessie. SCRAPPY becomes Jack again.)
BOFFO. Come on, Bessie, old girl. (To SCRAPPY.) Hey, buddy, here's your cow back.
DOXY. Moo! Moo!
SCRAPPY. But, sir, the beans you gave me grew and did bring me good fortune like you promised.
BOFFO. They did?
DOXY. Moo! Moo!
SCRAPPY. Couldn't you use Old Bessie in your circus act?
DOXY. Moo! Moo!
BOFFO. That's just it. Your talking cow won't talk any more!
DOXY. Moo! Moo!
SCRAPPY. Bessie, old girl, can't you talk any more?

CLOWNS' PLAY

DOXY. Of course I can, Jack. But that con man just wanted to use me. (She starts butting against BOFFO.) He's no good — a smooth-talking snake-in-the-grass. I'd like to ... (MOXY now becomes Mother again.)

SCRAPPY. Mother, look, Bessie's back! (To BOFFO.) You see, sir, Bessie's an independent cow — she only talks when she wants to! (BOFFO goes off.)

MOXY. Jack, we are most fortunate. Look at us. We have a talking cow ...

DOXY. Moo!

MOXY. We have a singing harp ... (TRINKET sings.) And we have our wonderful golden hen ...

MUSTARD. Cluck! Cluck!

SCRAPPY. Mother, maybe we can become clowns and have our own circus act! (MUSTARD breaks in. They are themselves — the CLOWNS again.)

MUSTARD. A most noble profession. (They come together in CLOWN pose.)

MUSCULO. Tremendous!

RUFFINA. Stupendous!

MOXY. Fascinating!

DOXY. Captivating!

SCRAPPY. Super!

BOFFO. And ... and ... (Trying to think of something.)

CLOWNS (together). And what?

BOFFO. Ah ... ah ... Fun!

MUSTARD. You said it. Come on, everyone, let's run out into the lobby and do the job they hired us to do — usher. (To audience.) Thank you for helping us play the story. We couldn't have done it without you. Come on — we'll meet you in the lobby. (The CLOWNS run down the aisles of the theatre out to the lobby where they will sign autographs and meet the audience. When the last member of the audience has gone, the Clowns' Play is over.)

PRODUCTION NOTES

The characters in the play are circus clowns, and they perform the business and wear the costumes of circus clowns. This is the motif out of which the story of *Jack and the Beanstalk* is eventually played. Everything from music to stage business should reflect this.

The part of Scrappy (Jack) is written to be played by a proficient mime. It should not be played by a child. The effect throughout should be of a group of clowns caught unaware by circumstances and using their wits and talents to improvise their way through the performance.

Participation is important to the action of the play. The audience must feel very much a part of the decisions the actors make, as well as in furthering the story. The actors should be alert to the audience and their responses and attempt to use their suggestions as much as possible.

Though lighting, sound effects and specific comic business are indicated in the text, the author does not feel these are absolutely necessary. They are indicated as suggestion and to serve as a spur of individual creative juices. Much of this can be tailored to the individual talents of the company, the space in which you are doing the play, and the age of your audience.

The approximate running time of the production is one hour.

PROPS NEEDED

Two signs on easels reading "Show Today — Jack and the Beanstalk."

A stick for a "sword" fight.

A piece of "steel" for Musculo to bend.

Water hose.

Wooden bucket filled with confetti.

Over-sized book with "Jack and the Beanstalk" clearly visible in large letters on the cover.

Hat with pieces of paper in it.

Blocks of various and assorted sizes.

Trunk filled with clown props — cap, jacket, apron, rope, cowbell, farmer's hat, small bag of money, bouquet of flowers, ax.

Ladder with a wire hooked to it.

Vine or garland.

"Magic" beans.

Over-sized pencil.

Long scroll.

Thunder sheet.

"Wind" sign.

PROPS (continued)

"Thunder" sign.

"Lightning" sign.

Giant's verse — Fee Fi Fo Fum etc. — on large cue card.

Bag of "gold."

Wheelbarrow.

Over-sized jar.

Large golden styrofoam "eggs."

SCRAPPY as Jack wears a cap and jacket.

MOXY as Mother wears an apron.

DOXY as Bessie the Cow wears a rope and cowbell. Cow-like eyelashes and a tail may be added but are not necessary.

MUSTARD as the Hen wears a brightly-colored coat with tails under which the eggs can be hidden. MUSCULO has a pouch tied around his neck, in which he keeps the secret formula for egg laying.

Cue card planted with member of the audience on which is written the secret formula for egg laying.

DIRECTORS NOTES

DIRECTORS NOTES